TABLE OF CONTENTS

Chicken Soup

6 cups chicken broth
1½ pounds boneless, skinless chicken
  breasts, cubed
2 cups sliced carrots
1 cup sliced mushrooms
1 red bell pepper, chopped

1 onion, chopped
2 tablespoons grated fresh ginger
3 teaspoons minced garlic
½ teaspoon red pepper flakes
  Salt and black pepper, to taste

Place all ingredients in **CROCK-POT®** slow cooker. Cover; cook on LOW 6 to 7 hours or on HIGH 3 to 3½ hours.

Makes 4 to 6 servings

Rich and Hearty Drumstick Soup

2 turkey drumsticks (about 1¾ pounds total)
2 medium carrots, sliced
1 medium stalk celery, thinly sliced
1 cup chopped onion
1 teaspoon minced garlic

½ teaspoon poultry seasoning
4½ cups chicken broth
2 ounces uncooked dry egg noodles
¼ cup chopped parsley
2 tablespoons butter
¾ teaspoon salt, or to taste

1. Coat **CROCK-POT®** slow cooker with nonstick cooking spray. Add drumsticks, carrots, celery, onion, garlic and poultry seasoning. Pour broth over; cover. Cook on HIGH 5 hours or until turkey meat is falling off bones.

2. Remove turkey; set aside. Add noodles to **CROCK-POT®** slow cooker; cover and cook 30 minutes more or until noodles are tender. Meanwhile, debone turkey and cut meat into bite-size pieces; set meat aside.

3. When noodles are cooked, stir in turkey, parsley, butter and salt.

Makes 4 servings

5

Cape Cod Stew

2 pounds shrimp, peeled, deveined and cleaned

2 pounds fresh cod or other white fish

3 lobsters (1½ to 2½ pounds each), uncooked

1 pound mussels or clams

2 cans (16 ounces each) chopped tomatoes

4 cups beef broth

½ cup chopped onions

½ cup chopped carrots

½ cup chopped cilantro

2 tablespoons sea salt

2 teaspoons crushed or minced garlic

2 teaspoons lemon juice

4 whole bay leaves

1 teaspoon dried thyme

½ teaspoon saffron

1. Cut shrimp and fish into bite-size chunks and place in large bowl; refrigerate. Remove lobster tails and claws. Chop tail into 2-inch pieces, and separate claws at joints. Place lobster and mussels in large bowl; refrigerate.

2. Combine remaining ingredients in **CROCK-POT®** slow cooker. Cover; cook on LOW 7 hours.

3. Add seafood. Turn **CROCK-POT®** slow cooker to HIGH. Cover; cook on HIGH 45 minutes to 1 hour or until seafood is just cooked through.

Makes 8 servings

Hamburger Veggie Soup

1 pound ground beef
1 bag (16 ounces) frozen mixed vegetables
1 package (10 ounces) frozen seasoning-blend vegetables
1 can (10¾ ounces) condensed tomato soup, undiluted

1 can (about 14 ounces) stewed tomatoes
2 cans (5½ ounces each) spicy vegetable juice
Salt and black pepper, to taste

Coat **CROCK-POT®** slow cooker with nonstick cooking spray. Crumble beef before placing in bottom. Add remaining ingredients. Stir well to blend. Cover; cook on HIGH 4 hours. If necessary, break up large pieces of beef. Add salt and pepper before serving, if desired.

Makes 4 to 6 servings

FAMILY FAVORITES

Pizza Soup

2 cans (about 14 ounces each) stewed
tomatoes with Italian seasonings

2 cups beef broth

1 cup sliced mushrooms

1 small onion, chopped

1 tablespoon tomato paste

¼ teaspoon salt, or to taste

¼ teaspoon black pepper, or to taste

½ pound turkey Italian sausage, casings
removed

Shredded mozzarella cheese

1. Combine tomatoes, broth, mushrooms, onion, tomato paste, salt and pepper in **CROCK-POT®** slow cooker.

2. Shape sausage into marble-size balls. Gently stir into soup mixture. Cover; cook on LOW 6 to 7 hours. Adjust salt and pepper, if necessary. Serve with cheese.

Makes 4 servings

Hearty Chicken Noodle Soup

1¼ pounds boneless, skinless chicken breasts

1¼ pounds boneless, skinless chicken thighs

12 baby carrots, cut into ½-inch pieces

4 stalks celery, cut into ½-inch pieces

¾ cup finely chopped onion

1 teaspoon dried parsley

½ teaspoon black pepper

¼ teaspoon ground red pepper

1 teaspoon salt

4 cans (about 14 ounces each) chicken broth

4 chicken-flavored bouillon cubes

2 cups uncooked egg noodles

1. Cut chicken into bite-size pieces. Place in **CROCK-POT®** slow cooker. Add carrots, celery, onion, parsley, black pepper, red pepper, salt, broth and bouillon cubes. Cover; cook on LOW 5 to 6 hours.

2. Stir in egg noodles. Turn **CROCK-POT®** slow cooker to HIGH. Cook 30 minutes longer or until noodles are tender.

Makes 8 to 10 servings

Mother's Sausage and Vegetable Soup

- 1 can (about 15 ounces) black beans, rinsed and drained
- 1 can (about 14 ounces) diced tomatoes
- 1 can (10¾ ounces) condensed cream of mushroom soup, undiluted
- ½ pound smoked turkey sausage, cut into ½-inch slices
- 2 cups diced potato
- 1 cup chopped onion
- 1 cup chopped red bell pepper
- ½ cup water
- 2 teaspoons extra-hot prepared horseradish
- 2 teaspoons honey
- 1 teaspoon dried basil

Combine all ingredients in **CROCK-POT®** slow cooker; mix well. Cover; cook on LOW 7 to 8 hours or until potato is tender.

Makes 6 to 8 servings

Potato Cheddar Soup

2 pounds new red potatoes, cut into ½-inch cubes
¾ cup coarsely chopped carrots
1 medium onion, coarsely chopped
½ teaspoon salt

3 cups chicken broth
1 cup half-and-half
¼ teaspoon black pepper
2 cups (about 8 ounces) shredded Cheddar cheese

1. Place potatoes, carrots, onion and salt in **CROCK-POT®** slow cooker. Pour in broth. Cover; cook on LOW 6 to 7 hours or on HIGH 3 to 3½ hours or until vegetables are tender.

2. Stir in half-and-half and pepper. Cover; cook on HIGH 15 minutes. Turn off heat and remove cover; let stand 5 minutes. Stir in cheese until melted.

Makes 6 servings

Serving Suggestion: *Try this soup topped with whole wheat croutons.*

Hearty Mushroom and Barley Soup

9 cups chicken broth
1 package (16 ounces) sliced mushrooms
1 onion, chopped
2 carrots, chopped
2 stalks celery, chopped
½ cup uncooked pearl barley

½ ounce dried porcini mushrooms
3 cloves garlic, minced
1 teaspoon salt
½ teaspoon dried thyme
½ teaspoon black pepper

Combine broth, sliced mushrooms, onion, carrots, celery, barley, dried mushrooms, garlic, salt, thyme and pepper in **CROCK-POT®** slow cooker. Cover; cook on LOW 4 to 6 hours.

Makes 8 to 10 servings

Variation: *For even more flavor, add a beef or ham bone to the CROCK-POT® slow cooker with the rest of the ingredients.*

Beef Fajita Soup

- 1 pound beef stew meat, cut into cubes
- 1 can (about 15 ounces) pinto beans, rinsed and drained
- 1 can (about 15 ounces) black beans, rinsed and drained
- 1 can (about 14 ounces) diced tomatoes with roasted garlic
- 1 can (about 14 ounces) beef broth
- 1½ cups water
- 1 green bell pepper, thinly sliced
- 1 red bell pepper, thinly sliced
- 1 onion, thinly sliced
- 2 teaspoons ground cumin
- 1 teaspoon seasoned salt
- 1 teaspoon black pepper

Combine beef, beans, tomatoes, broth, water, bell peppers, onion, cumin, salt and black pepper in **CROCK-POT®** slow cooker. Cover; cook on LOW 8 hours.

Makes 8 servings

Serving Suggestion: *Serve topped with sour cream, shredded Monterey Jack or Cheddar cheese and chopped olives.*

Italian Hillside Garden Soup

1 tablespoon extra-virgin olive oil
1 cup chopped green bell pepper
1 cup chopped onion
½ cup sliced celery
1 can (about 14 ounces) diced tomatoes with basil, garlic and oregano
1 can (about 15 ounces) navy beans, rinsed and drained
1 medium zucchini, chopped

1 cup frozen cut green beans, thawed
2 cans (about 14 ounces each) chicken broth
¼ teaspoon garlic powder
1 package (9 ounces) refrigerated sausage- or cheese-filled tortellini pasta
3 tablespoons chopped fresh basil
Grated Asiago or Parmesan cheese (optional)

1. Heat oil in large skillet over medium-high heat. Add bell pepper, onion and celery. Cook and stir 4 minutes or until onions are translucent. Transfer to **CROCK-POT®** slow cooker.

2. Add tomatoes, navy beans, zucchini, green beans, broth and garlic powder. Cover; cook on LOW 7 hours or on HIGH 3½ hours.

3. Add tortellini and cook on HIGH 20 to 25 minutes longer or until pasta is tender. Stir in basil. Garnish each serving with cheese.

Makes 6 servings

BEAN-BASED RECIPES

Penne Pasta Zuppa

1 can (about 15 ounces) white beans
2 medium yellow squash, diced
2 ripe tomatoes, diced
2 small red potatoes, cubed
2 leeks, sliced lengthwise into quarters
then chopped
1 carrot, diced
¼ pound fresh green beans, washed,
stemmed and diced

2 fresh sage leaves, minced
1 teaspoon salt
½ teaspoon black pepper
8 cups water
¼ pound uncooked penne pasta
Grated Romano cheese (optional)

1. Combine beans, squash, tomatoes, potatoes, leeks, carrot, green beans, sage, salt and pepper in **CROCK-POT®** slow cooker. Add water. Stir well to combine. Cover; cook on HIGH 2 hours, stirring occasionally. Turn **CROCK-POT®** slow cooker to LOW. Cook, covered, 8 hours longer. Stir occasionally.

2. Turn **CROCK-POT®** slow cooker to HIGH. Add pasta. Cover; cook on HIGH 30 minutes longer or until pasta is done.

3. To serve, garnish with Romano cheese.

Makes 6 servings

15

BEAN-BASED RECIPES

Hearty Lentil and Root Vegetable Stew

2 cans (about 14 ounces each) chicken broth

1½ cups turnips, cut into 1-inch cubes

1 cup dried red lentils, rinsed and sorted

1 medium onion, cut into ½-inch wedges

2 medium carrots, cut into 1-inch pieces

1 medium red bell pepper, cut into 1-inch pieces

½ teaspoon dried oregano

⅛ teaspoon red pepper flakes

1 tablespoon olive oil

½ teaspoon salt

4 slices bacon, crisp-cooked and crumbled

½ cup finely chopped green onions

1. Combine broth, turnips, lentils, onion, carrots, bell pepper, oregano and red pepper flakes in **CROCK-POT®** slow cooker. Stir to mix well. Cover; cook on LOW 6 hours or on HIGH 3 hours or until lentils are tender.

2. Stir in oil and salt. Sprinkle each serving with bacon and green onions.

Makes 8 servings

Fresh Lime and Black Bean Soup

2 cans (about 15 ounces each) black beans, undrained
1 can (about 14 ounces) chicken broth
1½ cups chopped onions
1½ teaspoons chili powder
¾ teaspoon ground cumin

¼ teaspoon garlic powder
⅛ to ¼ teaspoon red pepper flakes
½ cup sour cream
2 tablespoons extra-virgin olive oil
2 tablespoons chopped fresh cilantro
1 medium lime, cut into wedges

1. Coat **CROCK-POT®** slow cooker with nonstick cooking spray. Add beans, broth, onions, chili powder, cumin, garlic powder and red pepper flakes. Cover; cook on LOW 7 hours or on HIGH 3½ hours or until onions are very soft.

2. Process 1 cup soup mixture in blender until smooth and return to **CROCK-POT®** slow cooker. Stir, check consistency and repeat with additional 1 cup soup as desired. Let stand 15 to 20 minutes before serving.

3. Ladle soup into 4 bowls. Divide sour cream, oil and cilantro evenly among servings. Squeeze juice from lime wedges over each.

Makes 4 servings

Northwoods Smoked Ham and Bean Soup

2 tablespoons olive oil
2 large onions, chopped
6 cloves garlic, peeled and minced
6 cups chicken broth
2 smoked ham hocks
2 cups cubed cooked smoked ham
1 can (28 ounces) whole plum tomatoes, drained and coarsely chopped

1 bunch fresh parsley, stemmed and chopped
4 sprigs fresh thyme
4 whole bay leaves
2 cans (about 15 ounces each) cannellini beans, rinsed and drained
½ pound cooked orecchiette, cavatelli or ditalini pasta
  Kosher salt and black pepper

1. Heat oil in skillet over medium heat. Add onions and cook, stirring occasionally, until soft and fragrant, about 10 minutes. Add garlic and cook 1 minute.

2. Place onion and garlic mixture, broth, ham hocks, ham, tomatoes, parsley, thyme and bay leaves in **CROCK-POT®** slow cooker. Cook on LOW 10 hours or on HIGH 6 hours.

3. Stir in beans and pasta; continue to cook on HIGH until heated through.

4. Season to taste with salt and pepper and serve.

Makes 6 to 8 servings

BEAN-BASED RECIPES

Tuscan Bean and Prosciutto Soup

2 tablespoons unsalted butter
4 slices prosciutto*
3 cups water
1 cup dried navy beans, rinsed and sorted
½ cup dried lima beans, rinsed and sorted
1 medium yellow onion, finely chopped
1 tablespoon chopped fresh cilantro

1 teaspoon salt
1 teaspoon ground cumin
1 teaspoon black pepper
½ teaspoon ground paprika
2 cans (about 14 ounces each) diced tomatoes

Substitute 4 slices bacon, if desired.

1. Melt butter in large skillet over medium-high heat. Add prosciutto and fry until crisp. Remove to paper towels to cool.

2. Crumble prosciutto into small pieces in **CROCK-POT®** slow cooker. Add water, navy beans, lima beans, onion, cilantro, salt, cumin, pepper and paprika. Stir well to combine. Cover; cook on LOW 10 to 12 hours.

3. Add tomatoes; stir well. Turn **CROCK-POT®** slow cooker to HIGH. Cover; cook on HIGH 30 to 40 minutes or until soup is heated through.

Makes 6 servings

French Lentil Rice Soup

6 cups chicken broth or vegetable broth
1 cup lentils, rinsed and sorted
2 medium carrots, finely diced
1 small onion, finely chopped
2 stalks celery, finely diced
3 tablespoons uncooked white rice
2 tablespoons minced garlic

1 teaspoon herbes de Provence or dried thyme
½ teaspoon salt
⅛ teaspoon ground white pepper or black pepper
¼ cup heavy cream or sour cream (optional)
¼ cup chopped parsley (optional)

1. Stir together broth, lentils, carrots, onion, celery, rice, garlic, herbes de Provence, salt and pepper in **CROCK-POT®** slow cooker. Cover; cook on LOW 8 hours or on HIGH 4 to 5 hours.

2. Remove 1½ cups soup and process in blender or food processor until almost smooth.* Stir puréed soup back into **CROCK-POT®** slow cooker.

3. Divide soup evenly among four serving bowls. Garnish each serving with 1 tablespoon cream and 1 tablespoon chopped parsley, if desired.

Use caution when processing hot liquids in blender. Vent lid of blender and cover with clean kitchen towel as directed by manufacturer.

Makes 4 servings

BEAN-BASED RECIPES

Grandma Ruth's Minestrone

1 pound ground beef
1 cup dried red beans
1 package (16 ounces) frozen mixed vegetables
2 cans (8 ounces each) tomato sauce
1 can (about 14 ounces) diced tomatoes
¼ head shredded cabbage
1 cup chopped onions

1 cup chopped celery
½ cup chopped fresh parsley
1 tablespoon dried basil
1 tablespoon Italian seasoning
1 teaspoon salt
1 teaspoon black pepper
1 cup cooked elbow macaroni

1. Combine ground beef and beans in **CROCK-POT®** slow cooker. Cover; cook on HIGH 2 hours.

2. Add all remaining ingredients except macaroni and stir to blend. Turn **CROCK-POT®** slow cooker to LOW. Cover; cook on LOW 6 to 8 hours or until beans are tender.

3. Stir in macaroni. Turn **CROCK-POT®** slow cooker to HIGH. Cover; cook on HIGH 1 hour.

Makes 4 servings

Beef Stew with Bacon, Onion and Sweet Potatoes

1 pound beef stew meat, cut into 1-inch cubes

1 can (about 14 ounces) beef broth

2 medium sweet potatoes, cut into 2-inch chunks

1 large onion, cut into 1½-inch chunks

2 slices thick-cut bacon, diced

1 teaspoon dried thyme

1 teaspoon salt

¼ teaspoon black pepper

2 tablespoons cornstarch

2 tablespoons water

1. Coat **CROCK-POT®** slow cooker with nonstick cooking spray. Combine all ingredients except cornstarch and water in **CROCK-POT®** slow cooker; mix well. Cover; cook on LOW 7 to 8 hours or on HIGH 4 to 5 hours or until meat and vegetables are tender.

2. With slotted spoon, transfer beef and vegetables to serving bowl; cover with foil to keep warm.

3. Whisk cornstarch into water in small bowl. Stir into cooking liquid. Cover; cook on HIGH 15 minutes or until thickened. To serve, spoon sauce over beef and vegetables.

Makes 4 servings

Hearty Chicken Tequila Soup

1 small onion, cut into 8 wedges

1 cup frozen corn, thawed

1 can (about 14 ounces) diced tomatoes with mild green chilies

2 cloves garlic, minced

2 tablespoons chopped fresh cilantro, plus additional for garnish

1 whole fryer chicken (about 3½ pounds)

2 cups chicken broth

3 tablespoons tequila

¼ cup sour cream

1. Spread onions on bottom of **CROCK-POT®** slow cooker. Add corn, tomatoes, garlic and 2 tablespoons cilantro. Mix well to combine. Place chicken on top of tomato mixture.

2. Combine broth and tequila in medium bowl. Pour over chicken and tomato mixture. Cover; cook on LOW 8 to 10 hours.

3. Transfer chicken to cutting board. Remove skin and bones. Pull meat apart with two forks into bite-size pieces. Return chicken to **CROCK-POT®** slow cooker and stir.

4. Serve with dollop of sour cream and garnish with cilantro.

Makes 2 to 4 servings

Mexican Cheese Soup

1 pound pasteurized process cheese product, cubed

1 pound ground beef, cooked and drained

1 can (about 15 ounces) kidney beans, undrained

1 can (about 14 ounces) diced tomatoes with green chilies

1 can (about 14 ounces) stewed tomatoes, undrained

1 can (8¾ ounces) whole kernel corn, undrained

1 envelope taco seasoning

1 jalapeño pepper, seeded and diced* (optional)

Corn chips (optional)

Jalapeño peppers can sting and irritate the skin, so wear rubber gloves when handling peppers and do not touch your eyes.

1. Coat inside of **CROCK-POT®** slow cooker with nonstick cooking spray. Add cheese, beef, beans, tomatoes with chilies, stewed tomatoes, corn, taco seasoning and jalapeño pepper, if desired. Mix well.

2. Cover; cook on LOW 4 to 5 hours or on HIGH 3 hours or until done. Serve with corn chips, if desired.

Makes 6 to 8 servings

Squash and Beef Slow Cooker Stew

1 tablespoon vegetable oil
1 medium yellow onion, finely chopped
1 clove garlic, minced
2 cans (about 14 ounces each) diced tomatoes
2 cups 1-inch cubes butternut or buttercup squash (1 small squash)
1 pound beef stew meat, cut into bite-size cubes
1 can (about 15 ounces) butter beans, rinsed and drained

½ cup beef broth
1 teaspoon minced jalapeño pepper*
½ teaspoon salt
½ teaspoon dried oregano
½ teaspoon chili powder
¼ teaspoon ground cumin
¼ teaspoon black pepper

Jalapeño peppers can sting and irritate the skin, so wear rubber gloves when handling peppers and do not touch your eyes.

1. Heat oil in medium skillet over medium heat. Add onion and garlic; cook and stir 5 to 8 minutes or until onion is golden brown. (Do not let garlic burn.) Spoon onion and garlic into 5-quart **CROCK-POT®** slow cooker.

2. Add tomatoes, squash, beef, beans, broth, jalapeño pepper, salt, oregano, chili powder, cumin and black pepper to **CROCK-POT®** slow cooker. Cover; cook on HIGH 5 to 7 hours. Turn off heat. Let stew stand 30 minutes to thicken.

Makes 4 to 6 servings

Note: *To save time, skip step 1. Place raw onion and garlic in* **CROCK-POT®** *slow cooker. Add remaining ingredients and proceed as directed above.*

Curried Chicken and Coconut Soup

6 cups chicken broth

2 cans (13½ ounces each) unsweetened coconut milk

2 bunches green onions, sliced

3 to 4 tablespoons curry powder

4 stalks lemongrass, minced

2 tablespoons peeled and minced fresh ginger

8 large chicken thighs with bones, skin removed

2 packages (6 ounces each) baby spinach leaves

3 large limes, divided

Salt and black pepper, to taste

1 bunch chopped fresh cilantro

1. Combine broth, coconut milk, green onions, curry powder, lemongrass, ginger and chicken in **CROCK-POT®** slow cooker. Cook on LOW 10 hours or on HIGH 6 hours.

2. Remove chicken from **CROCK-POT®** slow cooker to cutting board; let rest for a few minutes.

3. Remove bones and cut chicken into ½-inch cubes. Return chicken to soup; add spinach. Cook on HIGH until spinach wilts, about 10 minutes. Juice 2 limes and add juice to **CROCK-POT®** slow cooker. Season soup to taste with salt and pepper. Cut remaining lime into 6 to 8 wedges. Ladle soup into individual serving bowls; sprinkle with cilantro and serve with lime wedges.

Makes 6 to 8 servings

Nana's Mini Meatball Soup

1 pound ground beef
1 pound ground pork
1½ cups finely grated Pecorino Romano or Parmesan cheese
1 cup Italian seasoned dry bread crumbs
2 eggs

1 bunch fresh Italian parsley
Kosher salt and black pepper
3 quarts chicken broth
1 bunch escarole, coarsely chopped
½ (16-ounce) package ditalini pasta, cooked and drained

1. Combine beef, pork, cheese, bread crumbs, eggs, parsley, salt and pepper in large bowl until well blended. Shape into ¾-inch meatballs.

2. Add meatballs and broth to **CROCK-POT®** slow cooker. Cover; cook on LOW 9 hours or on HIGH 5 hours.

3. Add escarole; cover and cook on LOW 15 minutes or until wilted. Stir in pasta just before serving.

Makes 6 to 8 servings

Tip: *You may substitute spinach for escarole, if desired.*

27

Sweet and Sour Brisket Stew

- 1 jar (12 ounces) chili sauce
- 1½ tablespoons packed dark brown sugar
- 1½ tablespoons fresh lemon juice
- ¼ cup beef broth
- 1 tablespoon Dijon mustard
- ¼ teaspoon paprika
- ½ teaspoon salt
- ¼ teaspoon black pepper
- 1 beef brisket, trimmed and cut into 1-inch cubes*

- 2 carrots, cut into ½-inch slices
- 1 onion, chopped
- 1 clove garlic, minced
- 1 tablespoon all-purpose flour (optional)

Beef brisket has a thick layer of fat, which some supermarkets trim off. If the meat is well trimmed, buy 2½ pounds; if not, purchase 4 pounds, then trim and discard excess fat.

1. Combine chili sauce, brown sugar, lemon juice, broth, mustard, paprika, salt and pepper in **CROCK-POT®** slow cooker.

2. Add beef, carrots, onion and garlic; mix well. Cover; cook on LOW 8 hours.

3. For thicker gravy, turn **CROCK-POT®** slow cooker to HIGH. Stir 3 tablespoons cooking liquid into flour in small bowl until smooth. Stir into **CROCK-POT®** slow cooker. Cover; cook on HIGH 10 minutes or until thickened.

Makes 6 to 8 servings

MEATY SOUPS & STEWS

Chuck and Stout Soup

2 tablespoons olive oil

3 pounds beef chuck roast, cut into 1-inch cubes

Kosher salt and black pepper

8 cups beef broth

3 onions, thinly sliced

3 stalks celery, diced

6 carrots, diced

4 cloves garlic, minced

2 packages (10 ounces each) cremini mushrooms, thinly sliced

1 package (about 1 ounce) dried porcini mushrooms, processed to a fine powder

4 sprigs fresh thyme

1 bottle (12 ounces) stout beer

Fresh Italian parsley (optional)

1. Heat oil in large skillet over medium-high heat. Season beef with salt and pepper. Working in batches, brown beef on all sides. Bring broth to a boil in large saucepan over high heat. Reduce heat to low; simmer until reduced by half.

2. Transfer beef to **CROCK-POT®** slow cooker. Add reduced broth and all remaining ingredients except parsley. Cover; cook on LOW 10 hours or on HIGH 6 hours.

3. Garnish with parsley just before serving, if desired.

Makes 6 to 8 servings

Note: *A coffee grinder works best for processing dried mushrooms, but a food processor or blender can also be used.*

CREAMY BOWLS

Celery-Leek Bisque

- 3 bunches leeks (about 3 pounds), trimmed and well rinsed
- 2 medium stalks celery, sliced
- 1 medium carrot, sliced
- 3 cloves garlic, minced
- 2 cans (about 14 ounces each) fat-free chicken broth
- 1 package (8 ounces) cream cheese with garlic and herbs
- 2 cups half-and-half, plus more for garnish
  Salt and black pepper, to taste
  Fresh basil (optional)

1. Combine leeks, celery, carrot, garlic and broth in **CROCK-POT®** slow cooker. Cover; cook on LOW 8 hours or on HIGH 4 hours.

2. Process mixture in blender, 1 cup at a time, until smooth, returning batches to **CROCK-POT®** slow cooker as they are processed. Add cream cheese to last batch in blender and process until smooth; stir cream cheese mixture and 2 cups half-and-half into soup. Add salt and pepper, to taste. Serve immediately, or cool to room temperature and refrigerate in airtight container (flavors intensify overnight). Reheat before serving. Garnish with additional half-and-half and basil leaves, if desired.

Makes 4 to 6 servings

Country Chicken Chowder

2 tablespoons butter or margarine
1½ pounds chicken tenders, cut into ½-inch pieces
2 onions, chopped
2 stalks celery, sliced
2 carrots, sliced

2 cups frozen corn
2 cans (10¾ ounces each) condensed cream of potato soup, undiluted
1½ cups chicken broth
1 teaspoon dried dill weed
½ cup half-and-half

1. Melt butter in large skillet over medium-high heat. Add chicken; cook and stir until browned.

2. Combine chicken, onions, celery, carrots, corn, soup, broth and dill weed in **CROCK-POT®** slow cooker. Cover; cook on LOW 3 to 4 hours or until vegetables are tender.

3. Turn off heat; stir in half-and-half. Cover; let stand 5 minutes or until heated through.

Makes 8 servings

Note: *For a special touch, garnish soup with croutons and fresh dill.*

Manhattan Clam Chowder

3 slices bacon, diced
2 stalks celery, chopped
3 onions, chopped
2 cups water
1 can (about 14 ounces) stewed tomatoes, undrained and chopped
4 small red potatoes, diced
2 carrots, diced

½ teaspoon dried thyme
½ teaspoon black pepper
½ teaspoon Louisiana-style hot sauce
1 pound minced clams*

If fresh clams are unavailable, use canned clams; 6 (6½-ounce) cans yield about 1 pound of clam meat. Drain and discard liquid.

1. Cook and stir bacon in medium saucepan until crisp. Remove bacon and place in **CROCK-POT®** slow cooker.

2. Add celery and onions to skillet. Cook and stir until tender. Place in **CROCK-POT®** slow cooker.

3. Mix in water, tomatoes, potatoes, carrots, thyme, pepper and hot sauce. Cover; cook on LOW 6 to 8 hours or HIGH 4 to 6 hours. Add clams during last half hour of cooking.

Makes 4 servings

Tip: *Shellfish and mollusks are delicate and should be added to the **CROCK-POT®** slow cooker during the last 15 to 30 minutes of the cooking time if you're cooking on HIGH, and during the last 30 to 45 minutes if you're cooking on LOW.*

Curried Sweet Potato and Carrot Soup

2 medium-to-large sweet potatoes, cut into ¾-inch dice (about 5 cups)

2 cups baby carrots

1 small onion, chopped

¾ teaspoon curry powder

½ teaspoon salt, or to taste

½ teaspoon black pepper, or to taste

½ teaspoon ground cinnamon

¼ teaspoon ground ginger

4 cups chicken broth

¾ cup half-and-half

1 tablespoon maple syrup

Candied ginger (optional)

1. Place sweet potatoes, carrots, onion, curry powder, salt, pepper, cinnamon and ground ginger in **CROCK-POT®** slow cooker. Add broth. Stir well to combine. Cover; cook on LOW 7 to 8 hours.

2. Process soup, 1 cup at a time, in blender, returning blended soup to **CROCK-POT®** slow cooker after each batch. (Or, use immersion blender.) Add half-and-half and maple syrup. Add salt and pepper, if desired. Turn **CROCK-POT®** slow cooker to HIGH. Cover; cook on HIGH 15 minutes to reheat. Serve in bowls and garnish with strips or pieces of candied ginger, if desired.

Makes 8 servings

Tip: *For richer flavor, add a teaspoon of chicken soup base along with broth.*

Creamy Farmhouse Chicken and Garden Soup

½ package (16 ounces) frozen pepper stir-fry vegetable mix

1 cup frozen corn

1 medium zucchini, sliced

2 bone-in chicken thighs, skinned

½ teaspoon minced garlic

1 can (about 14 ounces) fat-free chicken broth

½ teaspoon dried thyme

2 ounces uncooked egg noodles

1 cup half-and-half

½ cup frozen peas, thawed

2 tablespoons finely chopped fresh parsley

2 tablespoons butter

1 teaspoon salt

½ teaspoon black pepper

1. Coat **CROCK-POT®** slow cooker with nonstick cooking spray. Place stir-fry vegetables, corn and zucchini in bottom. Add chicken, garlic, broth and thyme. Cover; cook on HIGH 3 to 4 hours or until chicken is no longer pink in center. Remove chicken and set aside to cool slightly.

2. Add noodles to **CROCK-POT®** slow cooker. Cover; cook 20 minutes longer or until noodles are done.

3. Meanwhile, debone and chop chicken. Return to **CROCK-POT®** slow cooker. Stir in remaining ingredients. Let stand 5 minutes before serving.

Makes 4 servings

Double Corn Chowder

- **2** small stalks celery, trimmed and chopped
- **6** ounces Canadian bacon, chopped
- **1** small onion
- **1** serrano pepper, seeded and diced*
- **1** cup frozen corn, thawed
- **1** cup canned hominy
- **¼** teaspoon salt
- **¼** teaspoon dried thyme
- **¼** teaspoon black pepper, or to taste
- **1** cup chicken broth
- **1** tablespoon all-purpose flour
- **1½** cups milk, divided

Serrano peppers can sting and irritate the skin, so wear rubber gloves when handling peppers and do not touch your eyes.

1. Combine celery, bacon, onion, serrano pepper, corn, hominy, salt, thyme and black pepper in **CROCK-POT®** slow cooker. Pour in broth. Cover; cook on LOW 5 to 6 hours or on HIGH 3 to 3½ hours.

2. Stir together flour and 2 tablespoons milk in small bowl. Stir into corn mixture. Add remaining milk. Cover; cook on LOW 20 minutes.

Makes 4 servings

Tip: *For richer chowder, use ¼ cup milk and ¾ cup half-and-half.*

CREAMY BOWLS

Cauliflower Soup

2 heads cauliflower, cut into small florets
8 cups chicken broth
¾ cup chopped celery
¾ cup chopped onion

2 teaspoons salt
2 teaspoons black pepper
2 cups milk or light cream
1 teaspoon Worcestershire sauce

1. Combine cauliflower, broth, celery, onions, salt and pepper in **CROCK-POT®** slow cooker. Cover; cook on LOW 7 to 8 hours or on HIGH 3 to 4 hours.

2. Process soup until smooth using hand mixer or immersion blender. Add milk and Worcestershire sauce; process until blended. Cover; cook on HIGH 15 to 20 minutes or until heated through.

Makes 8 servings

ETHNIC TASTES

Greek Lemon and Rice Soup

3 cans (about 14 ounces each) chicken broth
½ cup uncooked long grain white rice (not converted or instant rice)
3 egg yolks
¼ cup fresh lemon juice

¼ teaspoon salt
⅛ teaspoon ground white pepper*
4 thin slices lemon (optional)
4 teaspoons finely chopped fresh parsley (optional)

Substitute ground black pepper, if desired.

1. Stir broth and rice together in **CROCK-POT®** slow cooker. Cover; cook on HIGH 2 to 3 hours or until rice is cooked.

2. Whisk egg yolks and lemon juice together in medium bowl. Whisk large spoonful of hot rice mixture into egg yolk mixture. Whisk back into **CROCK-POT®** slow cooker.

3. Turn **CROCK-POT®** slow cooker to LOW. Cover; cook on LOW 10 minutes. Season with salt and pepper. Ladle soup into serving bowls and garnish each bowl with thin slice of lemon and 1 teaspoon chopped parsley, if desired.

Makes 4 servings

Note: *Soup may be served hot or cold. To serve cold, allow soup to cool to room temperature. Cover and refrigerate up to 24 hours before serving.*

Vietnamese Chicken Pho

8 cups chicken broth
2 to 3 cups shredded cooked chicken
8 ounces bean sprouts
  Rice stick noodles

1 bunch Thai basil, chopped
  Hoisin sauce (optional)
  Lime wedges (optional)

1. Combine broth and chicken in **CROCK-POT®** slow cooker. Cover; cook on LOW 6 to 7 hours or on HIGH 3 hours.

2. Add bean sprouts, noodles and Thai basil. Cover; cook until noodles are softened.

3. Spoon soup into individual serving bowls and serve with hoisin sauce and lime wedges, if desired.

Makes 4 to 6 servings

Note: *A simple soup to prepare with leftover shredded chicken, this classic Asian chicken noodle soup packs tons of flavor.*

Irish Stew

1 cup fat-free reduced-sodium chicken broth
1 teaspoon dried marjoram
1 teaspoon dried parsley flakes
¾ teaspoon salt
½ teaspoon garlic powder
¼ teaspoon black pepper

1¼ pounds white potatoes, cut into 1-inch pieces
1 pound lean lamb for stew, cut into 1-inch cubes
8 ounces frozen cut green beans, thawed
2 small leeks, cut lengthwise into halves, then crosswise into slices
1½ cups coarsely chopped carrots

1. Combine broth, marjoram, parsley, salt, garlic powder and pepper in **CROCK-POT®** slow cooker; mix well.

2. Layer potatoes, lamb, green beans, leeks and carrots in **CROCK-POT®** slow cooker. Cover; cook on LOW 7 to 9 hours or until lamb is tender.

Makes 6 servings

Tip: *If desired, thicken cooking liquid with a mixture of 1 tablespoon cornstarch and ¼ cup water. Stir mixture into cooking liquid; cook on HIGH 10 to 15 minutes or until thickened.*

Mediterranean Shrimp Soup

2 cans (about 14 ounces each) fat-free reduced-sodium chicken broth
1 can (about 14 ounces) diced tomatoes
1 can (8 ounces) tomato sauce
1 medium onion, chopped
½ medium green bell pepper, chopped
½ cup orange juice
½ cup dry white wine (optional)
1 jar (2½ ounces) sliced mushrooms

¼ cup sliced pitted black olives
2 cloves garlic, minced
1 teaspoon dried basil
2 whole bay leaves
¼ teaspoon whole fennel seeds, crushed
⅛ teaspoon black pepper
1 pound medium raw shrimp, peeled and deveined

1. Place all ingredients except shrimp in **CROCK-POT®** slow cooker. Cover; cook on LOW 4 to 4½ hours or until vegetables are crisp-tender.

2. Stir in shrimp. Cover; cook 15 to 30 minutes or until shrimp are pink and opaque. Remove and discard bay leaves.

Makes 6 servings

Note: *For a heartier soup, add 1 pound of firm white fish (such as cod or haddock), cut into 1-inch pieces, 45 minutes before end of cooking time.*

ETHNIC TASTES

Linguiça & Green Bean Soup

1 large yellow onion, chopped
3 cloves garlic, minced
2 tablespoons olive oil
1 cup tomato juice
4 cups water
1 tablespoon Italian seasoning
2 teaspoons garlic salt
1 teaspoon ground cumin

1 whole bay leaf
2 cans (16 ounces each) cut green beans, drained
1 can (about 15 ounces) kidney beans, drained
1 pound linguiça sausage links, fried until cooked through, then cut into bite-size pieces

1. Place all ingredients in **CROCK-POT®** slow cooker. Cover; cook on LOW 8 to 10 hours or on HIGH 4 to 6 hours. Add more boiling water during cooking, if necessary.

2. Remove and discard bay leaf before serving. Serve with warm cornbread.

Makes 6 servings

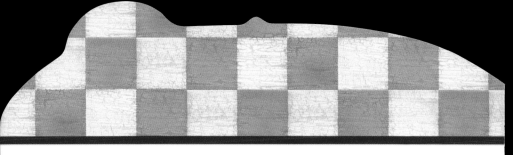

Fiesta Black Bean Soup

6 cups chicken broth
12 ounces potatoes, peeled and diced
1 can (about 15 ounces) black beans, rinsed and drained
½ pound cooked ham, diced
½ onion, diced
1 can (4 ounces) diced whole green mild chilies

2 cloves garlic, minced
2 teaspoons dried oregano
1½ teaspoons dried thyme
1 teaspoon ground cumin
Sour cream, chopped bell pepper and chopped tomatoes (optional)

1. Combine broth, potatoes, beans, ham, onion, chilies, garlic, oregano, thyme and cumin in **CROCK-POT®** slow cooker; mix well. Cover; cook on LOW 8 to 10 hours or on HIGH 4 to 5 hours.

2. Adjust seasonings. Serve with desired toppings.

Makes 6 to 8 servings

Asian Beef Stew

2 onions, cut into ¼-inch slices

1½ pounds boneless beef round steak, sliced thin across the grain

2 stalks celery, sliced

2 carrots, sliced

1 cup sliced mushrooms

1 cup orange juice

1 cup beef broth

⅓ cup hoisin sauce

2 tablespoons cornstarch

1 to 2 teaspoons Chinese five-spice powder or curry powder

1 cup frozen peas

Hot cooked rice

Chopped fresh cilantro (optional)

1. Layer onions, beef, celery, carrots and mushrooms in **CROCK-POT®** slow cooker.

2. Combine orange juice, broth, hoisin sauce, cornstarch and five-spice powder in small bowl. Pour into **CROCK-POT®** slow cooker. Cover; cook on HIGH 5 hours or until beef is tender.

3. Stir in peas. Cover; cook on HIGH 20 minutes or until peas are tender. Serve over rice. Garnish with cilantro, if desired.

Makes 6 servings

Russian Borscht

4 cups thinly sliced green cabbage

1½ pounds fresh beets, shredded

5 small carrots, halved lengthwise and cut into 1-inch pieces

1 parsnip, peeled, halved lengthwise and cut into 1-inch pieces

1 cup chopped onion

4 cloves garlic, minced

1 pound beef stew meat, cut into ½-inch cubes

1 can (about 14 ounces) diced tomatoes

3 cans (about 14 ounces each) reduced-sodium beef broth

¼ cup lemon juice, or to taste

1 tablespoon sugar, or to taste

1 teaspoon black pepper

Sour cream (optional)

Chopped fresh parsley (optional)

1. Layer cabbage, beets, carrots, parsnip, onion, garlic, beef, tomatoes, broth, lemon juice, sugar and pepper in **CROCK-POT®** slow cooker. Cover; cook on LOW 7 to 9 hours or until vegetables are crisp-tender.

2. Season with additional lemon juice and sugar, if desired. Dollop each serving with sour cream and sprinkle with parsley, if desired.

Makes 12 servings

Tortilla Soup

2 cans (about 14 ounces each) chicken
  broth
1 can (about 14 ounces) diced tomatoes
  with jalapeño peppers
2 cups chopped carrots
2 cups frozen corn, thawed
1½ cups chopped onions

1 can (8 ounces) tomato sauce
1 tablespoon chili powder
1 teaspoon ground cumin
¼ teaspoon garlic powder
2 cups chopped cooked chicken (optional)
  Shredded Monterey Jack cheese
  Crushed tortilla chips

1. Combine broth, tomatoes, carrots, corn, onions, tomato sauce, chili powder, cumin and garlic powder in **CROCK-POT®** slow cooker. Cover; cook on LOW 6 to 8 hours.

2. Stir in chicken, if desired. Ladle into bowls. Top each serving with cheese and tortilla chips.

Makes 6 servings

Minestrone alla Milanese

2 cans (about 14 ounces each) reduced-sodium beef broth
1 can (about 14 ounces) diced tomatoes
1 cup diced red potatoes
1 cup coarsely chopped carrots
1 cup coarsely chopped green cabbage
1 cup sliced zucchini
¾ cup chopped onion
¾ cup sliced fresh green beans
¾ cup coarsely chopped celery

¾ cup water
2 tablespoons olive oil
1 clove garlic, minced
½ teaspoon dried basil
¼ teaspoon dried rosemary
1 whole bay leaf
1 can (about 15 ounces) cannellini beans, rinsed and drained
Shredded Parmesan cheese (optional)

1. Combine all ingredients except cannellini beans and cheese in **CROCK-POT®** slow cooker; mix well. Cover; cook on LOW 5 to 6 hours.

2. Add cannellini beans. Cover; cook 1 hour or until vegetables are tender.

3. Remove and discard bay leaf before serving. Top with Parmesan cheese, if desired.

Makes 8 to 10 servings